OPENING DOORS

Senior Authors
Carl B. Smith
Ronald Wardhaugh

Macmillan Publishing Co., Inc.
New York

Collier Macmillan Publishers
London

SERIES **r** ™
Macmillan Reading

This work is also published in individual volumes under
the titles: *Amigos* and *Ups and Downs*, copyright © 1980
Macmillan Publishing Co., Inc. Parts of this work were
published in SERIES ⌈: The New Macmillan Reading Pro-
gram.

Macmillan Publishing Co., Inc.
866 Third Avenue, New York, New York 10022
Collier Macmillan Canada, Ltd.

Printed in the United States of America
ISBN 0-02-128330-3
98765432

ACKNOWLEDGMENTS

The publisher gratefully acknowledges permission to reprint the following copyrighted material:

"The Donkey Knows," adapted from "I Think I Know," in *Fried Onions And Marshmallows* by Sally Melcher Jarvis. Text copyright © 1968 by Sally Jarvis. By permission of Parents' Magazine Press.

"I Wish I Had a Diamond," by Richard Ulloa, from *Wishes, Lies And Dreams* by Kenneth Koch. Copyright © 1970 by Kenneth Koch. Used by permission of Chelsea House Publishers, New York.

"I Woke Up One Morning," from *A Rumbudgin of Nonsense* by Arnold Spilka. Copyright © 1970 by Arnold Spilka. Reprinted by permission of Arnold Spilka.

"I wonder how it feels to fly . . .," adapted from *The Turquoise Horse* edited by Flora Hood. Copyright © 1972 by Flora Hood. Reprinted by permission of G.P. Putnam's Sons and Curtis Brown, Ltd.

"If I Were a . . .," from *The Rose On My Cake* by Karla Kuskin. Copyright © 1964 by Karla Kuskin. By permission of Harper & Row, Publishers, Inc.

"Look," from *All That Sunlight* by Charlotte Zolotow. Text copyright © 1967 by Charlotte Zolotow. By permission of Harper & Row, Publishers, Inc.

"Mouse Wants a Friend," adapted from *Mouse Looks For A Friend* by Helen Piers. Copyright © 1966 by Helen Piers. Reprinted by permission of Methuen Children's Books and Franklin Watts, Inc.

"The Secret Place," from *All Together* by Dorothy Aldis. Copyright 1925, 1927, 1928, 1934, 1939, 1952 by Dorothy Aldis. Reprinted by permission of G.P. Putnam's Sons.

"Silly Sam," adapted from *Silly Sam* by Leonore Klein. Copyright © 1969 by Scholastic Magazines, Inc. Reprinted by permission of Scholastic Magazines, Inc.

"Slow Pokes," by Laura Arlon, from *Humpty-Dumpty's Magazine,* September, 1955. Reprinted by permission of Laura Arlon.

"Things in the Pool," from *Little Raccoon and Poems From The Woods* by Lilian Moore. Copyright © 1975 by Lilian Moore. Used with permission of McGraw-Hill Book Company.

"Things That Go Together," from *Just Think!* by Betty Miles and Joan Blos. Copyright © 1971 by Betty Miles. Reprinted by permission of Alfred A. Knopf, Inc.

"Tree House," from *Where the Sidewalk Ends* by Shel Silverstein. Copyright © 1974 by Shel Silverstein. By permission of Harper & Row, Publishers, Inc.

"The Wheels of the Bus Go Round and Round," from *Finger Play* by Mary Miller and Paula Zajan. Copyright © 1955 by G. Schirmer, Inc. Used by permission.

"Izzy," from *Where's Izzy?* by Jeannette McNeely. Copyright © 1972 by Jeannette McNeely. Reprinted by permission of Follett Publishing Company division of Follett Corporation.

"Who Is So Pretty?" from *Mouse Chorus* by Elizabeth Coatsworth. Copyright © 1955 from Pantheon Books, Inc. Reprinted by permission of Pantheon Books, a Division of Random House, Inc.

Illustrations: Frank Bozzo, Richard Brown, Kevin Callahan Carveth, Olivia Cole, Tom Cook, Ray Cruz, Lewis Friedland, Les Gray, Don Leake, Liebert Studios, Kenneth Longtemps, Sal Murdocca, Stacy Rogers, Joanne Scribner, Bob Shein, Jozef Sumichrast, Susan Swan, Sims Taback, Philip Wende, Jerry Zimmerman **Photographs:** T. Crissinger, James Foote, Beryl Goldberg, Norman Owen Tomalin (Bruce Coleman Inc.) **Cover Design:** AKM Associates

Contents

8

AMIGOS

"Amigos" is a word
that says friends.
Who are your friends?
What do you and
your friends like to do?

As you read "Amigos,"
see if the friends
do things that you do.

Who Is So Pretty?

Skitter, skatter,
Leap and squeak!
We've been dancing
Half the week.

Under the sofa,
Along the shelf,
Every mouse
Is wild as an elf.

Big round ear
And bright black eye,
Nimble and natty,
Limber and spry—

Who is so pretty,
Who is so neat,
As a little mouse dancing
On little gray feet?

—Elizabeth Coatsworth

Mouse Wants a Friend

Helen Piers

Part One
Who Can Be a Friend?

Mouse wants a friend.
He wants a friend
who can run and jump.

Can he be a friend?
No.
He can't run and jump.
He likes to sit and look.

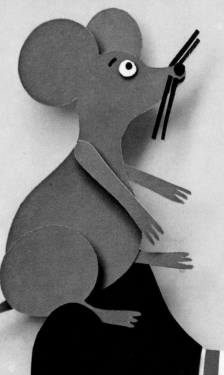

13

Can he be a friend?
No.
He can't run and jump.
He likes to fly.

14

Can he be a friend?

NO!

15

Mouse wants a friend
who does not sit and look.
He wants a friend
who does not fly.
Mouse wants a friend
who can run and jump.

16

Part Two
Mouse Finds a Friend

Can he be a friend?

No.

He can't run.

He can jump.

But he jumps high.

He jumps too high.

17

Can he be a friend?
No.
He can't run and jump.
He likes to walk slowly.
He walks too slowly.

Mouse wants to find a friend.
But he does not like
to sit and look.
He can't fly or jump high.
And he does not like
to walk slowly.
Will Mouse
find a friend?

Look!
What is that?

Does she jump up and down?
Yes!

Does she run in and out?
Yes!

Is she the friend Mouse wants?

20

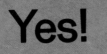

Yes!

She is a mouse, too.

Write a Word

Look at the letters in the box.
Find the letters that make
the words go with the pictures.
Write the words on your paper.

a	e	i	o	u

1. c a n

2. b o x

3. h a t

4. s u n

5. n a t

6. p i g

Find the letter that makes a word.
Write the word on your paper.
Then write the sentence.

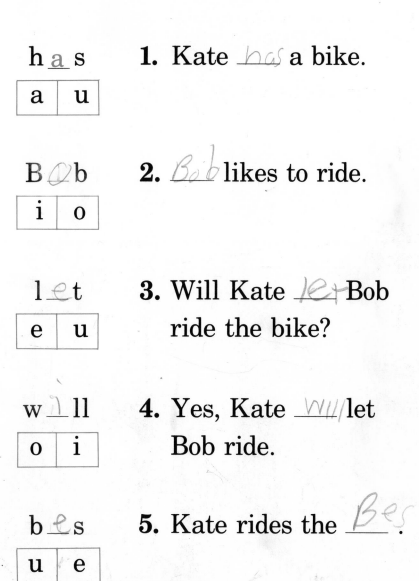

h <u>a</u> s
a	u

1. Kate _has_ a bike.

B _o_ b
i	o

2. _Bob_ likes to ride.

l <u>e</u> t
e	u

3. Will Kate _let_ Bob
ride the bike?

w <u>i</u> ll
o	i

4. Yes, Kate _will_ let
Bob ride.

b <u>e</u> s
u	e

5. Kate rides the _Bes_ .

The Happy Woman

Dina Anastasio

Part One
The School Bus

I went to school on a bus.
My friends went on the bus, too.
We liked to ride
on the school bus.

SCHOOL BUS

24

A happy woman drove the bus.
We liked the happy woman
who drove the bus.
She drove and she sang.
She sang to the birds.
She sang to the dogs.
She sang to my friends.
And we sang, too.

The woman gave funny presents
to my friends and me.
And we gave funny presents
to the woman.

I gave little things,
like a little mouse
and a little car.

She liked the car.
She liked the mouse, too.

26

Part Two
A Sad Day

One day the happy woman
was not on the bus.

A new woman drove the bus that day.
The new woman was not too happy.

We sang to the new woman.
But she said,
"I don't like that.
You can't do that on the bus."

I said to the new woman,
"Where is my friend
who drove the bus?"

The new woman said,
"She is too old.
She is at home."

"I want to see her.
She is my friend," I said.

So one day I went
to find the old woman.
I went to her house.
The old woman was not there.
But a little girl was there.

I said, "Where is the woman
who likes boys and girls?"

"She is at the park with her dog.
You will find her there,"
said the girl.

I went to the park,
but she was not there.

A woman was there.
But she was not my friend.

So I went home.
"I can't find the happy old woman,"
I said.

I was sad that day.
The old woman was my friend.

Part Three
The Old Woman at School

One day I went to school.
And there was the old woman!

"Are you going to drive the bus?"
I said.
"Are you going to drive
my friends and me home?"

"No," said the woman.
"I can't drive the bus.
But I can do other work.
I will see if I can find
other work here."

I went into school.

"The old woman is here,"
I said to my friends.
"She is here to find work."

My friends said,
"She is too old.
She can't work here."

"She can if she wants to,"
I said.

In school we read,
and we sang.
But the day went slowly.

Then we went to the lunchroom.
And there she was!
The old woman!

"Are you going to work here?"
I said.

"Yes," she said.
"I like it here in the lunchroom.
I can be with my friends."

So the old woman worked
in the lunchroom.
"I like to be
with my friends," she said.
"And they like to be
with me, too."

The Wheels of the Bus

The wheels of the bus go round and round
Round and round, round and round.
The wheels of the bus go round and round
All through the town.

Go Round and Round

The people on the bus go up and down
Up and down, up and down.
The people on the bus go up and down
All through the town.

The kids on the bus go *yakkity-yak*
Yakkity-yak, yakkity-yak.
The kids on the bus go *yakkity-yak*
All through the town.

— *Anonymous*

41

Suzy's Day

Here is what Suzy does one day.

42

Read the sentences.
They say what Suzy does.

> • Suzy is going
>   to the lunchroom.
> • Suzy sits down
>   and looks at pictures.
> • Suzy jumps up.

1. On your paper, write the sentence
   that says what Suzy does first.
2. Write the sentence that
   says what she does next.
3. Then write the sentence that
   says what Suzy does last.

In School Again

Sally R. Bell

It is the first day of school.
Boys and girls go to school again.
They see friends.
They work.
There are many things to do.
It is the first day of school.

44

There are new boys and girls
in the school.
They may not know where to go.
They may be lost in school.
They may not have friends.
They will find new friends.

Other boys and girls help
the new boys and girls.
They will help with the work.
They will be new friends.

46

There is time to read in school.
There is time to paint.
There is time to play, too.
Boys and girls do many things
in school.

Soon it is time to go home.
Boys and girls find their things.
They go out of the school.
They go with their new friends.
The boys and girls go home.
They will go to school again
on other days.

48

There will be many things for boys and girls to do. They like to go to school.

I wish I had a diamond
I wish I had a bike
I wish I had a cat
I wish I had a puppy
I wish I had a friend.

—Richard Ulloa
Grade One

50

51

The House in the Woods

Judith Adams

Part One
A Place for Things

There was a hill in the woods.
There was a house on the hill.
And there was a man in the house.
The man liked things to be in place.

He liked to know
where to find his hat
and where to find his umbrella.
He liked to know
where to find his other things.

So there was a place for his hat
and a place for his umbrella.
And there was a place for
his other things, too.

"I like to know where things
are," said the man.

Part Two
The Green Rock

The man was happy with his things.
And he was happy to have a house
in the woods.

One day he went out for a walk
in the woods.
The woods were green.

"What a day!" said the man.

He looked at the woods.
There were birds that sang.
There was a little lake.
There were fish in the lake.

The man saw the birds fly.
And he saw the fish jump.
And he liked what he saw.

Then the man looked down.
And he saw a rock.
It was a green rock,
and he liked it.

"It will go with my things,"
said the man.
"I will find a place for it
if I can."

He looked at the woods.
He saw the fish and the birds.
And he saw his green rock.
The man was happy.

"What a day!" he said.

Part Three
A Surprise

"Will my green rock go here?"
said the man.

But the rock looked too big.
It did not go there.

"Will it go here?"

But the rock looked too little.
It did not go there.

"I like this rock," said the man.
"But if there is no place for it,
I can't have it in my house.
Out you go."

But then he looked at the rock.
"What is this?" he said.
"A turtle! A surprise!
A green turtle!
What a surprise!"

"This turtle can be my friend.
Can I find a place for a friend
in my house?"

The man looked at his hat box.
Then he looked at the box
for his other things.

"My hat does not have to have a box,"
he said.
"It can go with my other things."

"This box will be for you,"
the man said to the turtle.
"There is a place for my things
and a place for you!"

And the man and the turtle
were happy in the house
on the hill in the woods.

63

Slow
Pokes

Turtles are slow,
As we all know.
But
To them
It is no worry,

For
Wherever they roam,
They are always at home,
So
They do not
HAVE
To hurry.

— LAURA ARLON

Izzy

Jeannette McNeely

Part One
Where Is Izzy?

Hal looked in the box.
Mindy looked, too.

"Izzy was in this box.
He is not here.
Where is Izzy?" said Hal.

"Does your mother know?
Did you ask your mother?"
said Mindy.

"No!" said Hal.
"If I ask my mother, she will
want me to do my school work."

"Does your father know?
Did you ask your father?"
Mindy said.

"No!" said Hal.
"If I ask my father, he will
want me to paint the house."

"Did you ask that man?"
said Mindy.

"No!" said Hal.
"He will want my help."

"Did you ask that woman?"
said Mindy.

"No!
She will want my help, too."

Then Mindy said,
"I know what you can do, Hal.
You can ask and run!"

"Why do you say that?" said Hal.

"If you ask and run,
then you don't have to help,"
said Mindy.

71

"Yes!" said Hal.
"That is what I will do."
"Hal! Hal!" said Mindy.

But Hal was not there.

Part Two
Hal Runs Fast

Hal ran to the house.

He saw his mother.
"Have you seen Izzy?" Hal said
as he ran.

"No, Hal, but—"
Hal ran fast.
"Hal!" said his mother.

But he was gone.

He saw his father.

"Have you seen Izzy?"
Hal said as he ran.

"No, Hal.
But—"

Hal ran fast and was gone.

Hal saw the man.
"Have you seen Izzy?" said Hal
as he ran.

"No," said the man.
Then he looked up.
"Hal—"

But Hal ran too fast for the man.

Hal saw the woman.

"Have you seen Izzy?" said Hal.

"No," said the woman.

"Is—?"

But Hal ran fast and was gone.

Part Three
Hal Finds Izzy

Hal saw the mail carrier.
"Have you seen Izzy?" said Hal.

"Who is Izzy?"
said the mail carrier.

"Izzy is my lizard,"
Hal said.

"He is, is he?"
the mail carrier said.

"Yes, Izzy is my lizard.
But where is he?" Hal said.

"Hal, come here,"
said the mail carrier.
"Is this lizard Izzy?"

"Yes!" said Hal.
"This is Izzy!"

Part Four
Hal and Izzy

"I see you found your lizard,"
said the woman.
"I wanted to tell you,
but you ran too fast."

"I see you found your lizard,"
said the man.
"I wanted to tell you,
but you ran too fast."

"I see you found your lizard,"
said Mindy.
"I wanted to tell you,
but you ran too fast."

Hal and the mail carrier
laughed.

83

Hal saw his father.

"I see you found Izzy,"
his father said.
"I wanted to tell you, but—"

"I know.
I ran too fast."
Hal laughed.

Hal went to the house.

"I see you found Izzy," said his mother.

"I know," Hal said. "You wanted to tell me, but I ran too fast."

"No," said his mother. "I wanted to tell you to do your school work!"

"Mother!" said Hal.

Then he looked at Izzy, and he laughed.

85

Word Surprise

Find the letter or letters in a box
to make the picture word.
Write the word on your paper.

b	t	k

1. <u>b</u> ag

fl	dr	pr

2. _fl_ ag

r	m	s

3. ___ ip

fr	dr	sl

4. _dr_ ip

s	b	r

5. _r_ ide

sl	br	gr

6. _sl_ ide

Find the letter or letters in a box
to make a new word.
Write the sentence on your paper.

1. I see a <u>bat</u>.
   Can it fly into a <u>h</u>at?

h	s	t

2. Go down on your <u>sled</u>.
   Then come to <u>b</u>ed.

m	g	b

3. See the rain <u>drip</u>.
   Don't you <u>sl</u>ip.

sl	pr	fr

4. Have a <u>ride</u>.
   Come to the <u>sl</u>ide.

fl	sl	fr

5. See that man in <u>red</u>.
   He looks like <u>Fl</u>ed.

Fl	Pr	Fr

6. Get a <u>grip</u>.
   Do a <u>fl</u>ip.

fr	fl	pr

Here I Come

Judith Adams

Part One
A Day for the Park

Debbie and Ann are friends.
If it does not rain,
the girls like to go to the park.

One day Ann said,
"Debbie, Debbie, come on out.
This is a day for the park.
That's the place to go."

Debbie looked out.
"It looks like a day for the park,"
she said.
"I'll be out.
Wait for me."

"Ann, wait for me!"
It was a boy.

"Who is that?" said Debbie.

"That's Jay," said Ann.
"His mother and my mother
are friends."

The boy ran up to the girls.

"Do you want to come
 to the park?" said Ann.

"That's the place to be
on a day like this," said Jay.
"I'll come."

"Run and hide," said Ann.
"Then I'll find you."

"I like to hide," said Debbie.
"Come on, Jay."

"I like to hide, too," said Jay.
"Wait and see.
I'll hide so Ann can't find me!"

Jay and Debbie ran to hide.

Part Two
One, Two, Three

One.
Two.
Three.
Here I come!

Ann looked for Jay
and Debbie.
She saw a box.
She looked in.
But she did not see
Jay or Debbie.

92

Then she saw a red thing.

"That's a red hat," said Ann.
"Jay had his red hat on.
That's Jay!"

"I see you, Jay.
Come out.
Come out,
and I'll look for Debbie,"
said Ann.

"I saw you peek," said Jay.
"You saw me run and hide.
That's what you did."

"I did not peek," Ann said.
"I saw your red hat.
But hide if you want to.
I'll call one, two, three.
Then I'll look for you."

"Wait here," said Jay as he ran.
"And don't peek!"

One.
Two.
Three.
Here I come.

Ann looked in the box again.
But no one was there.
She looked and looked.
She saw a big rock.
Then she saw the red hat
move.

It was Jay!
Ann didn't see Debbie.

"Come out, Jay," Ann said.

"You said one, two, three too fast."
Jay said.
"So I didn't hide where I wanted to.
And that's why you found me.
I want to hide again."

Ann was not happy with Jay.
But she said, "Hide again.
You can hide where you want to.
Let's see if I can find you."

One.
Two.
Three.
Here I come.

Ann looked and looked.
Then she looked up.
She saw a red thing move.
It was Jay with his red hat
again.

But Ann didn't call Jay.

She went to look for Debbie.
She looked and looked.
And then she saw her.

"Come out, Debbie.
I found you," said Ann.
"I saw you move.
I know where Jay is, too.
But he likes to hide.
So he can hide!
Let's go."

The two girls went to the lake.

"Where is Ann?" said Jay.
"I don't want to wait here.
I'll see where she is."

Jay went to the lake.
"Ann," he said.
"I wanted you to find me."

"I did," said Ann.
"But you didn't like it.
So I let you hide."

Jay was happy to be
with his friends again.
He likes to hide sometimes.
But he didn't hide again that day!

The Secret Place

Halfway up a certain tree
There's a place belongs to me,
Two branches make a little chair
And I like it sitting there.

I like it.
And it's a secret too.
No grownup guesses where I go.
And if he should, and climbed to it—
He would not fit, he would not fit!

—DOROTHY ALDIS

AMIGOS

The friends in "Amigos"
did many things.
They worked and played.

Thinking About "Amigos"

1. Why did Mouse want to find
   a friend?
2. Why did the little girl
   want to find her friend
   who drove the bus?
3. What will the new boys
   and girls do in school?
4. What things did the friends
   in "Amigos" do that you do, too?

UPS AND DOWNS

Sometimes you help your family.
You help your friends work and play.
Your family and friends help you, too.
Many of the friends in "Ups and Downs"
help each other.
Other friends can't help each other.

As you read, look for friends
who can help each other.
Look for other friends
who don't help each other.

Things in the Pool

In this quiet pool
fish
glide
bugs
ride
snakes
slide
turtles
hide.

And in this quiet place
I
see
Me
looking up,
my
eyes
my
face.

—Lilian Moore

107

The Elves and the Shoemaker

Part One
Fred and Kate

There was a shoemaker and his wife.

The shoemaker was Fred.

His wife was Kate.

They had a little house.

They liked their house.

Fred liked to make shoes.
He liked to make shoes
for boys and girls.

Fred wanted leather to make shoes.
He had to have money for leather,
but Fred and Kate had no money.
So Fred and Kate were sad.

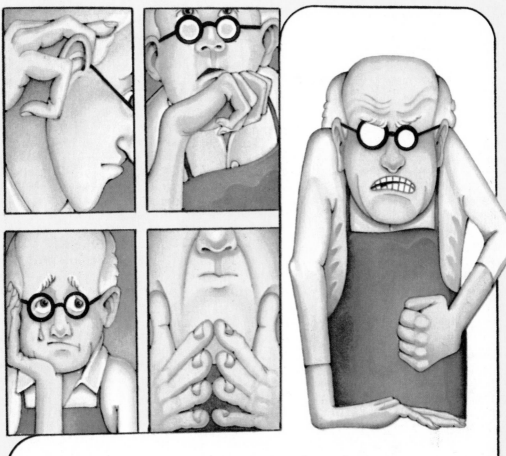

Fred did have a little leather.

He had leather for two shoes.

He cut it up.

Fred put the leather on his table.

He looked at the leather.

He had to have new leather!

Part Two
The Shoes

In the morning,

Fred went to make the shoes.

He looked at his table.

The shoes were made!

Who had made the shoes?

Fred and Kate didn't know.

But a man liked the shoes.

The man gave money to Fred.

Fred got new leather.
Now Fred and Kate were happy.
Fred cut up the leather.
He put it on his table.

It was morning.

Fred and Kate got up.

They looked at the table.

The shoes were made again!

Boys and girls liked the shoes.

They gave money to Fred.

Each day, Fred got new leather.

He cut it up.

He put it on his table.

Each morning, the shoes were made.

Boys and girls liked the shoes.

They gave money to Fred.

Fred and Kate were happy.

Part Three
The Elves

One day, Fred said,
"I want to know
who makes the shoes.
Let's hide.
Then we can see who it is."
Kate said, "I like that.
We will hide."
So they went to hide.

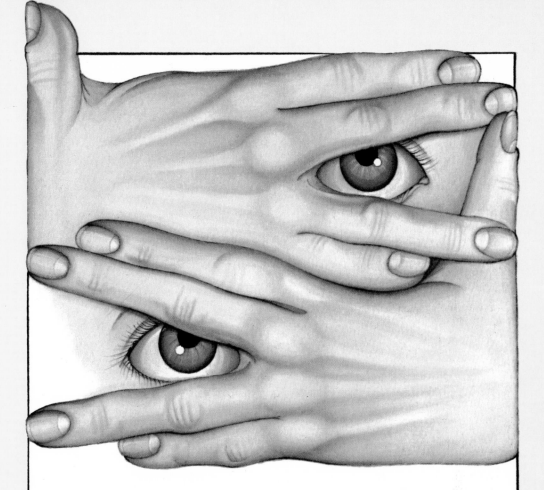

Fred and Kate had to wait and wait.

Then they saw a funny thing.

Elves were in the house!

The elves went to the table.

They made the shoes.

Then the elves went out of the house.

In the morning, Kate said,
"I want to make a present
for the elves.
I will make new hats for the elves."
Fred said, "I like that.
I will make new shoes for the elves."
So Fred and Kate worked and worked.

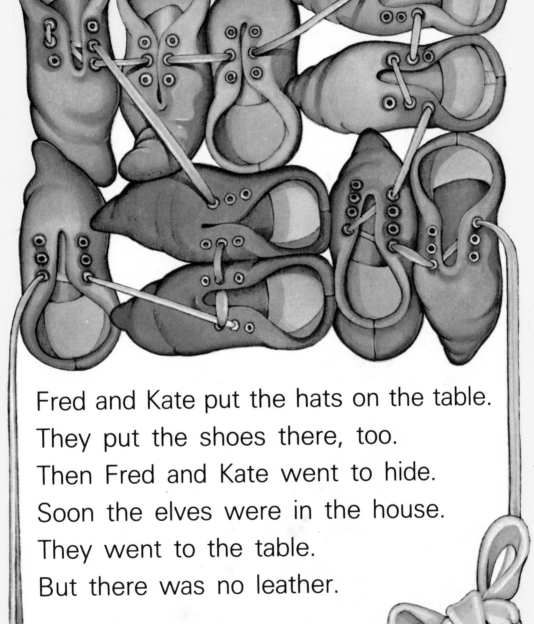

Fred and Kate put the hats on the table.

They put the shoes there, too.

Then Fred and Kate went to hide.

Soon the elves were in the house.

They went to the table.

But there was no leather.

119

The elves saw the new hats.

They saw the new shoes.

The elves liked the new things.

They put on the hats and shoes.

The elves sang and laughed.

The elves were happy.

They ran out of the house.

The elves didn't come again.
But Fred and Kate were happy.
Fred and Kate had money
for new leather.
So Fred made many new shoes.

The Magic e

What letter makes a word to name
each picture?
Write each word on your paper.

| a | i | o |

1. b_i_ke

2. l__ke

3. h__me

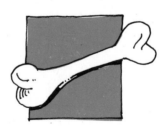

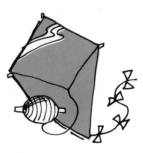

4. c__ke

5. b__ne

6. k__te

What letter makes a word that can
go in each sentence?
Write each sentence on your paper.

a	i	**1.** Mindy wanted to h__de.
o	a	**2.** Kate dr__ve to the park.
a	i	**3.** Jay played a g__me.
i	a	**4.** We can m__ke a bird happy.
o	i	**5.** I can tell the t__me.
o	a	**6.** Ann g__ve Grandma a picture.
a	o	**7.** We can walk h__me.

Put two words in a sentence.
Write each sentence on your paper.

a	o	**8.** We dr__ve to the pl__ce.
a	i	**9.** Hal g__ve his w__fe a present.
i	a	**10.** Kim will r__de to the l__ke.

I woke up one morning

Without any head,

So I jumped to the floor

And looked under the bed,

Then under my pillow,

The table,

The chair,

But look where I would,

My head wasn't there.

Not on the ceiling,
Not on the floor,
Not in the tree,
Not near the door.
Then at last I remembered—
Sure enough, just like that,
I found my old head!
It was under my hat.

—Arnold Spilka

125

A SURPRISE FOR GRANDMA

Lenore Israel

**Part One
Fun
With
Grandma**

"We will be gone
for two days,"
said Mother.
"Grandma will
take care of you girls.
And she will
take care of the house."

"What can we do?"
asked Linda and Myra.

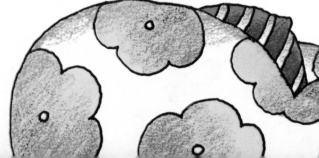

126

"You can be good girls," said Father.
"And you can have fun.
You can play and ride your bikes.
Grandma will take care of things."

The family said good-by.
Then Mother and Father were gone.

Grandma said to the girls,
"I like fun, too!
Linda, you take your red bike.
Myra, you take your green bike.
And I'll take the old bike
with no paint on it.
Let's ride to the park."

128

In the park Grandma said,
"I have a ball with me.
Let's play and have fun."

The two girls played ball
in the park with Grandma.

Then Grandma said,
"Let's ride home again.
Let's see who
can get there first."

129

Grandma got home first.
"It looks like rain," she said.

"Let's run to the house,"
said Linda.

"I like to run," said Myra.

"Me, too," said Grandma.
"Let's run!"

Part Two
The Girls Take Care of Things

In the morning Grandma said,
You girls go out and have fun.
I will sit in the house.
That will help my cold."

Linda and Myra were going out to play.
Then Linda said,
"Grandma wants to take care
of her cold.
Who will take care of things
in the house?"

Linda looked at Myra.
And Myra looked at Linda.

"We will," said the girls.

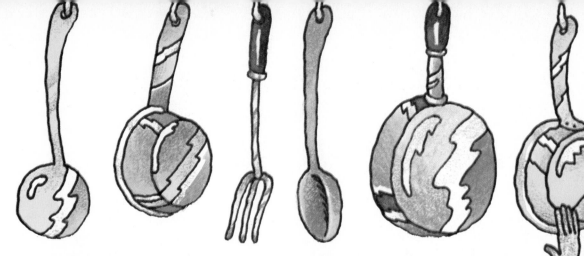

"What can we do to help?" asked Myra.

"Grandma will want to eat lunch,"
said Linda.
"So we can be the cooks this morning!
Come on.
I'll find a pot to cook lunch in."

"And I'll find things to cook,"
said Myra.

133

"Look!

I found a fish," said Myra.

"And here are two eggs."

"Fish and eggs go into the pot,"
said Linda.

"And here is a can of soup,"
said Myra.

"Soup into the pot!" said Linda.

"Fish and eggs and soup," said Linda.
"Lets' find one other thing to cook."

Myra looked and looked.
And then she said,
"I know!
Ice cream!
I love ice cream."

"Ice cream into the pot!" said Linda.

135

"Fish and eggs and soup for lunch,"
said Linda.

"And ice cream!" said Myra.
"What a surprise for Grandma!"

Grandma looked at her lunch,
and she laughed.
"This is a surprise!" she said.

Part Three
Mother and Father Come Home

Linda, Myra, and Grandma
were playing ball again.
A car
drove up.

137

"Mother! Father!"
said Linda and Myra.

"I didn't think you liked to play ball,"
said Father to Grandma.

"But I do," said Grandma.
"And I love playing with the girls.
Linda and Myra were
a big help to me, too.
Tell what you did today, girls."

"Grandma wanted to take care
of her cold today," said Linda.
"So Myra and I gave her lunch."

"What did you cook for Grandma?"
asked Mother.

"We cooked something good,"
said Myra.
"When you have a cold,
we will cook something good for you."

"I think I'll like that," said Mother.

Grandma and the girls laughed.

If I Were a Sandwich

If I were a sandwich,
I'd sit on a plate
And think of my middle
Until someone ate
Me.
End of the sandwich.

—Karla Kuskin

John's Day

Norah Smaridge

Part One
John's Morning

It was a bad morning for John.
He looked at his frog,
and he looked at his things.
There were his crayons.
There were his paints.
And there was his boat.
But he was not happy,
and his things didn't help.

142

His mother looked at John.
"You don't look happy to me,"
she said.
"Why don't you play
with your crayons or your paints?"

"I don't want to.
That's why!" said John.

"Then why not take your frog
and go find Liza?" said his mother.

"No!" said John.
"Liza ran when she saw
my frog this morning.
She said she didn't like it."

"This **is** a bad morning for you,"
said his mother.
"Why don't you..."

But John didn't wait.
He ran out of the house
with his things.
And then—
he threw his boat
into the garbage can!

Liza was there,
and she saw what John did.

"Don't do that, John!
I love that red boat!" said Liza.

"I can do what I like
with my things," said John.
"**Look.**"

He threw his paints
into the garbage can.
He threw his crayons in, too.
Then he laughed.

"That's not funny, John!" she said.

"I think it is," said John.
"Go home, Liza,
or **you** will go
into the garbage can, too."

Liza wanted to play with John.
But she saw it was a bad morning.
So she went home.
And John ran to the park.

146

Part Two
John's Afternoon

John ran into the park.
He thought of the morning.
He thought of the things
he threw out.
He thought of Liza.

He saw two little boys
with a big box.

The text on the box reads: FRAGILE THIS SIDE UP-FRAG

"Let's break it," said one.
"Yes, let's break it," said the other.

John ran to the box.

"Don't break that box.
We can make a house
out of it," said John.
"Help me take it home."

148

John went home with the boys
and the box.

In the afternoon John looked
in the garbage can.
There were his paints
and his crayons.

"I'll paint the house," John said.
"And you can make windows."

"Let's make big windows,"
said the two little boys.

Mother saw the house.

"I love the windows!" she said.
"I'll make you a door.
Then you can go in."

When there was a door,
the boys went into the house.
And so did John's frog.

Then a girl looked in
the door.
It was Liza.

"You can't come in," said John.
"My frog is in here with me.
And you don't like it."

"John, I have your boat,"
said Liza.
"And I have a fly
for your frog, too.
But you can't have your boat
or the fly if I can't come in!"

John looked at his frog,
and he looked at Liza.

Then he said,
"Come in, Liza.
Come in."

It was a bad morning.
But it was a good afternoon.

154

I wonder how it feels to fly
high in the sky . . .
   like a bird.

I wonder how it feels to sit
on a nest . . .
   like a bird.

I wonder how it feels to catch
a worm in the morning . . .
   like a bird.

I feel funny . . .
maybe it is wondering
   how it feels to be like a child.

—*Yakima*

155

Silly Sam

Leonore Klein

Part One
A Fish for Alice

Silly Sam was going to a party.

It was a party for Alice.

He put on his shoes.

He put on his hat.

He put on his coat.

And he went to the party.

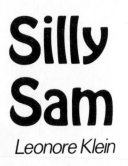

Silly Sam went by a man
with a fish.

"I am going to a party for Alice,"
said Silly Sam.
"Do you know what present
I can give her?
She has books and hats
and balls and crayons.
She has all kinds of things
to play with.
What present can I give her?"

"Does she have a fish
that can jump up and down?"
asked the man.

"No," said Silly Sam.

"I will give you a fish
that can jump up and down,"
said the man.
"Stop by a lake and put in the fish.
He will jump up and down.
But you have to give me your shoes."

Silly Sam wanted a present
for Alice.
So he gave the man his shoes.

Silly Sam went by a lake.

"I will stop and put in the fish,"
said Silly Sam.
"I want to see it jump
up and down."

Silly Sam put in the fish.

"Jump!" he said.

But the fish did not jump.
Sam looked, and the fish was gone.
"Stop!" called Silly Sam.
But the fish did not stop.

"What will I do?"
said Silly Sam.
"Alice has all kinds of things
to play with.
I have no present for her.
And I have no shoes."

Part Two
The Fly That Was Not There

Silly Sam went on his way.
He saw a boy with a box.

"I will stop and ask this boy
if he can help me," said Silly Sam.

"I am on my way to a party
for Alice," said Silly Sam.
"Do you know what
present I can give her?
She has books and hats
and balls and crayons.
She has all kinds
of things to play with."

"Does she have a fly
that no one can see?"
asked the boy.

"No," said Silly Sam.

"I will give you a fly
that no one can see," said the boy.
"But you have to give me your hat."

Silly Sam wanted a present
for Alice.
So he gave the boy his hat.

Silly Sam wanted to see the fly.
So he looked in the box.
But he didn't see a fly.
He looked and looked.
But there was no fly in the box.

"What will I do?" said Silly Sam.
"I have no present for Alice.
I have no shoes, and I have no hat."

Silly Sam went on his way.

Part Three
Good-by, Bird

Silly Sam saw a little girl
with a gold cage.
There was a gold bird in the cage.

"I am on my way to a party
for Alice," said Silly Sam.
"Do you know what present
I can give her?
She has books and hats
and balls and crayons.
She has all kinds of things
to play with."

"Does she have a bird
that can fly very high?"
asked the little girl.

"No," said Silly Sam.

"I will give you a bird
that can fly very high.
But you have to give me your coat."

Silly Sam wanted a present
for Alice.
So he gave the girl his coat.

Silly Sam wanted to see
the bird fly very high.
So he looked in the gold cage.
And the bird flew out.
It flew up high.
It flew up very high.
Then it flew away.

"What will I do?" said Silly Sam.

"I have no present for Alice.

The fish did not jump up and down.

There was no fly in the box.

The bird flew away.

And I gave away my shoes, my hat, and my coat."

Part Four
At the Party

Silly Sam was very sad.
He looked back at the cage.
Then he looked back
at the cage again.
And he saw a little gold egg.

"I will go to the party," said Silly Sam.
"And I will give Alice this egg.
I have no other present for her."

The girls and the boys at the party
laughed at Silly Sam.
There he was
without shoes,
without a hat,
and without a coat on his back.
And the boys and girls laughed
at his little present, too.

But Alice looked at the egg.
And, as she looked, it cracked.
And then it cracked a little more.
And then it cracked a little more.

There, in the egg,
was a little gold bird.
It was a little gold bird
for Alice.

"A gold bird!" said Alice.
"I love my present, Sam.
I do!"

Silly Sam had no shoes.
He had no hat.
And he had no coat.
But he didn't care.
He had a happy friend.

174

Things That Go Together

Thunder and lightning go together.
So do hands and mittens,

Beans and rice, fire and ice,
Mother cats and kittens.

News and weather go together.
So do reading and writing,
Fish and bones!
Ice cream and cones!
Also, loving and fighting.

Betty Miles and Joan Blos

175

What Is the Question?

Sentences that ask something are called question sentences.
Write the question sentences on your paper.

1. Is it John's surprise party?

1. Is it John's surprise party?

2. Alice had fun at the party.

3. Did Linda come to the party?

4. Kate can ride her bike to the party.

5. Did John want all his friends at the party?

6. Who will come to the party?

7. We ate ice cream at the party.

8. Do you like ice cream?

9. Did Sam have a present?

A sentence that asks something must
have a question mark at the end.
Write the sentences that must
have question marks.
Then put the question mark in
each sentence.

1. Do you love your grandma

    1. Do you love your grandma?

2. I love my grandma

3. Where is my grandma

4. Grandma is my friend

5. Did Myra cook an egg

6. Myra cooks an egg each day

7. Who cooked an egg

8. Ben eats ice cream each day

9. Who eats ice cream each day

10. Does Ben eat ice cream

11. Sam had a happy friend

Rosa and Her Shadow

Judith Adams

When Rosa goes out to play,

she is not alone.

Her shadow is there.

She can't go out without it.

Or can she?

She puts on her hat and goes out.

Rosa is quiet, very quiet.

She thinks she is alone.

Then she slowly looks back.

And what does she see?

Her shadow!

She was so quiet, too.

178

Rosa takes her time as she walks.
And her shadow takes its time, too.
Then she sees her friends
and she runs.
And her shadow runs
to be there with her.

When Rosa goes home to eat,
she is not alone.
Her shadow is there all the time.

What if Rosa wants to be alone?
She can't put her shadow in a box.
And she can't give it away.
How **do** you say good-by to a shadow?

DO YOU KNOW?

Look

Firelight and shadows
dancing on the wall.
Look at my shadow
TEN FEET TALL!

—Charlotte Zolotow

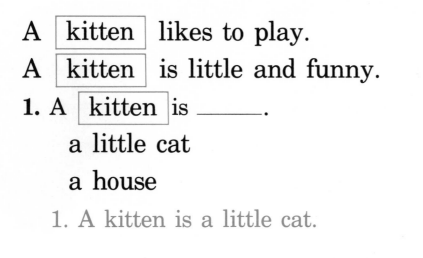

Think!

Look at the word in the box.
Think what the word in the box means.
Write each sentence on your paper.

A ❘ kitten ❘ likes to play.
A ❘ kitten ❘ is little and funny.
1. A ❘ kitten ❘ is _____.

    a little cat

    a house

   1. A kitten is a little cat.

A ❘ dictionary ❘ is something you can read.
A ❘ dictionary ❘ tells about words.
2. A ❘ dictionary ❘ is _____.

    a lizard

    a book

A   pond   has frogs in it.

You can fish in a   pond   .

3. A   pond   is _____.

    a small lake

    a crayon

A   canary   can fly.

A   canary   can be in a cage.

4. A   canary   is _____.

    a little bird

    a green bike

A   cafeteria   is a place to eat.

People have lunch in a   cafeteria   .

5. A   cafeteria   is _____.

    a pony

    a lunchroom

The Donkey Knows

The Players:

Donkey

Donkey Man

Walking Man

Time: **Day**

Place: **A country road**

Sally Melcher Jarvis

*(Walking Man is walking
down the road.
Donkey Man rides down
the road on his donkey.)*

Walking Man: This is a hot day.
It is too hot to walk.
*(He sees Donkey Man
on his donkey.)*
Will you give me a ride?
I will give you money.

189

Donkey Man: Yes!
Give me your money.

Walking Man: Here you are.
*(He gives Donkey Man money,
and he jumps on Donkey.)*

Donkey Man: How hot it is!
I think I will stop for water.

Donkey: *(to himself)*
Will they think of me?
*(Walking Man and Donkey Man
stop for water.
They don't give water to Donkey.)*

191

Donkey: *(to himself)* I am hot,
but they didn't give me water.

Walking Man: I think I will sit down.

Donkey: *(to himself)*
Can't I sit down, too?

Walking Man: It is so hot!
I think I will sit
in the shadow of the donkey!

Donkey Man: No, you don't!

There is a place for one man here.

It is **my** donkey.

I think I will sit in his shadow.

Walking Man: I gave you money.

I will sit there!

(He sits down in the shadow of Donkey.)

Donkey Man: You gave me money
to ride my donkey.
You didn't give me money
to sit in his shadow.
I will sit there!
*(He pushes Walking Man
out of the shadow.)*

Walking Man: Don't do that!
(*He pushes Donkey Man,
and he pushes Donkey.*)

Donkey: (*to himself*)
I think I will run away!
(*He runs away.*)

Donkey Man: Come back! Come back!

Walking Man: He is gone!

Donkey Man: It is so hot.
And we have to walk.
There is no shadow for you
or for me.

Walking Man: Why do you think the donkey
ran away?

Donkey Man: I don't know.

Walking Man: And **I** don't know.

Donkey: *(He is down the road.*
He looks back.)
I know why!

197

Tree House

A tree house, a free house,
A secret you and me house,
A high up in the leafy branches
Cozy as can be house.

A street house, a neat house,
Be sure and wipe your feet house
Is not my kind of house at all —
Let's go live in a tree house.

—Shel Silverstein

UPS AND DOWNS

In "Ups and Downs," you read about
friends who helped each other.
They helped each other do things
and find things.
You read about friends who didn't
help each other, too.

Thinking About "Ups and Downs"

1. How did the elves
   help Fred and Kate?
2. What did the girls do
   to help their Grandma?
3. Why do you think Donkey Man
   and Walking Man didn't help Donkey?
4. What things do you do to help
   your family and friends?

Word List

9. Amigos
   friends
   as
   if
12. mouse
    wants
    friend
    be
    no
16. *not*

17. finds
    high
18. slowly
19. *find*
20. she
    yes
22. write
    letters
    box
    make
    pictures
    paper

23. *letter*
    makes
    sentence
24. happy
    woman
    school
    went
    liked
25. drove
    sang
26. gave

To the Teacher: The words listed beside the page numbers above are introduced in *Opening Doors*. The children should be able to use previously taught skills to identify the italicized words independently.

27. day
was
new
29. said
old
want
her
30. there
34. going
drive

35. other
work
here
37. *read*
38. lunchroom
39. worked
they
42. Suzy's
43. *sentences*
first
next
last

44. again
many
45. know
46. help
47. time
play
48. soon
their
days
49. for
52. place
53. his

55. green
    rock
    were
56. looked
    saw
59. surprise
60. this
61. turtle
66. Izzy
    Hal
    Mindy

67. mother
    ask
68. father
73. fast
    ran
    seen
74. gone
77. mail
    carrier
    lizard

81. four
    found
    wanted
    tell
83. laughed
86. *picture*
87. *rain*
88. Debbie
    Ann
    that's
    I'll
    wait

90. Jay

91. *hide*

93. *thing*

    had

94. peek

96. move

97. didn't

    let's

101. *let*

    sometimes

104. played

    thinking

    about

105. ups

    downs

    each

108. elves

    shoemaker

    Fred

    wife

109. shoes

110. leather

    money

111. *cut*

    put

    table

112. morning

    made

113. *got*

122. *name*

123. *Grandma*

126.	*take*	129.	ball	135.	ice
	care		*get*		cream
	asked	131.	cold		love
	Linda	133.	eat	137.	playing
	Myra		lunch	138.	think
127.	good		cooks		today
	fun		*pot*	139.	*cooked*
	bikes		*cook*		something
	good-by	134.	eggs		when
128.	*bike*		soup		

142. John's	149. windows	157. by
bad	150. door	*am*
John	156. silly	give
frog	Sam	has
crayons	Alice	books
boat	coat	*balls*
143. Liza		all
144. threw		kinds
garbage		158. stop
147. afternoon		must
thought		161. *called*
148. break		162. way

166. gold	177. *asks*	180. *takes*
cage	mark	its
167. very	end	182. how
168. flew	*marks*	186. means
away	178. Rosa	187. *book*
170. *back*	shadow	188. donkey
egg	goes	*knows*
171. *without*	alone	players
172. cracked	*puts*	*walking*
more	quiet	road
176. question	*thinks*	189. *hot*

190. *gives*

191. water

himself

194. pushes

200. *helped*